Published by Izzy and Jack
www.izzyandjack.co.uk

Sunny

By Mary Rasamny

Illustrated by Izzy Bean

This book is dedicated to the newest Little
People with so much love to:

Dottie, Zade, Bodhi,
Casey and Kaia.

Should you find me, my name is Sunny.
A silver band is on my leg.

I'm a cinnamon pied cockatiel;
two ounces soaking wet.

I'm a precious little ball of yellow feathers
and soft grey down.

With rosy cheeks, big wide feet
and wispy feathers on my crown.

If you see me please bring me home
to the only place I've ever known.

Where Mom strokes my neck
and rubs my cheeks against her face.

And Dad lets me sit with him
in his favorite chair place.

Although I have a special crate
that is tall, deep and wide

with pretty toys, tinkling bells,
a shiny mirror inside,

I like to sit way up high
on my perch and look out

at the trees and the deer
and squirrels running about.

Against my mirror is where I snuggle
when the day becomes night

And my crate is closed tight
as Dad turns out the light

'til Mom's in the kitchen saying
"Morning, Sunny!" opening my door

so I can help toast her muffins
and her coffee we pour.

She lets me dip my beak
in her cup for just a sip.

And she holds me so my head
is tilted forward against her lips.

And then she kisses me and tells me
I'm such a good little bird

while the dogs bark for attention,
loudest noise you ever heard!

I'm on my own each day sitting high,
looking out everywhere.

All alone but Tuesdays and Fridays
when Maria is there.

She lets me sit on her shoulder
while she scrubs and cleans with me.

I hate the noise of the vacuum
but I love her company.

And next thing I know
my Mom's walking through the door!

I'm chirping my very loudest
and Jazzy's barking even more.

And it's "Hi Sunny, Hi Jazzy,
Hi Lulu -I'll be right there!"

As I fly to her shoulder,
careful not to land in her hair.

She lets me nibble on her earring
and the necklace 'round her neck

as she's making the salad
and gives me lettuce to peck.

There's a bowl of fresh water
always out for me to drink

and a bigger bowl for bathing
which she keeps by the sink.

I'm sorry I broke your heart
when I flew out the door that day.

I was looking through the glass -
I didn't mean to run away!

But the sun was shimmering off the leaves
and the sky was so blue.

I had to go, to explore!
I never wanted to leave you!

Peering up in the branches
I heard you calling my name

hour after hour
as the sun began to wane.

So I thought I should answer,
to let you know I was free!

But you thought I needed help
to come down from that tree.

So every time you called up to me
I chirped back down to you.

And Dad with his loud voice,
"Come Sunny!" was out there too.

I saw my crate wide open
as though expecting me to fly in

and sip my water, nibble seeds,
like what had happened had never been.

But I had to be free,
that's why God gave me wings.

You decided not to clip them,
you let me try out those things.

And as I grew older and bolder
I yearned for what I spied

through the family room window:
a great, green world, open wide.

I'll be just fine – I'll make friends
and eat leaves on the trees.

I'll sip water with the others
in shallow puddles and sparkling streams.

I'll snuggle up to some tree bark
to keep warm in the night.

I'll think of you lots
but please know I'm alright.

And if you see a flash of yellow
or hear what sounds like my cry,

please know I'm just checking in
and saying, Mom and Dad, goodbye.

And don't you worry about the weather,
for you know with my feathers I'll be safe,
warm and dry

with my new flock of friends
where my world never ends.

Printed in the USA
CPSIA information can be obtained
at www.ICGtesting.com
LVHW081333190823
755607LV00004B/154